From the Flyers Novice AE Team

# Thanks To My Hockey Dad

To All Hockey Dads with Love and Thanks

Toronto, Ontario, Canada

The publisher gratefully acknowledges the support of the Canada Council for the Arts and the Ontario Arts Council for its publishing program. We acknowledge the support of the Government of Ontario through the Ontario Media Development Corporation's Ontario Book Initiative.

We acknowledge the financial support of the Government of Canada through the Book Publishing Industry Development Program (BPIDP) for our publishing activities.

KPk is an imprint of
Key Porter Books Limited
Six Adelaide Street East, Tenth Floor
Toronto, Ontario, Canada  M5C 1H6

www.keyporter.com

Printed and bound in Canada
09 10 11 12 13 5 4 3 2 1

Library and Archives Canada Cataloguing in Publication

Thanks to my hockey dad / Flyers Novice AE Team.

ISBN 978-1-55470-283-1

1. Hockey players--Family relationships--Ontario--Orangeville.
2. Fathers and sons.  I. Flyers Novice AE Team (Hockey Team)

GV848.5.A1T39 2009          796.962092'271341          C2009-904722-5

this book is dedicated
to all
hockey dads
with love and thanks.

contributors Cade B, Cameron M,
Carter T, Conner H, Dawson C, Ethan D, Ethan S,
Harrison M, Jacob S, Liam M, Myles H, Ranen D,
Richard W, Trevor A, Zach V

# introduction

Being a hockey coach has provided me with the opportunity to teach—and learn from—some wonderful kids over the years. I have looked forward with anticipation to every game and practice, and savoured every moment: every win, every loss. I have also really enjoyed seeing the parents interacting with their children. Through the unique and very honest window that coaching sports opens, I have had a chance to witness these special relationships—intimate moments of loving, praising, scolding, teaching, and dreaming. There is almost no limit to what hockey parents will do for their kids.

And I guess that's how this project got started with our Novice rep team—I wanted to do something nice for the parents, for a change, on behalf of their kids. I wanted to do something that would give the kids an opportunity to show (and feel) appreciation, in this case for their dads.

With the help of a teacher, Jennifer Sutoski—who just happens to be the mom of one of our players—the project got underway. Jennifer worked with the players and encouraged them to think about their dads, and to remember the things for which they should be thankful. Their words, and the pictures they drew to accompany them, are honest, touching, surprising, and funny. I hope you enjoy them as much as we do.

The players remind us, with that special wisdom that only children seem to possess, that each moment is a memory to be filed away forever. These kids know what their dads have done for them—the efforts have not gone unnoticed.

Not surprisingly, I've been thinking about my own dad. If there is one thing I can be thankful for, and there are many, I wouldn't point to a single skill he taught me or piece of advice he offered—instead, I am thankful for the fact that he left it all up to me. He let me be a kid. And the kid chose to become a coach. Thanks, Dad!

jason howell Flyers Novice AE Coach

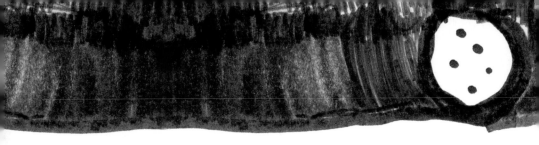

I remember my first set of skates: They were in the window of a shoemaker's shop, they had white tape on the toes, and I thought they were so cool. My Dad bought them for me. You never forget your first skates.

I remember my Mom waking me up at five in the morning, calling "Donald, Donald" quietly so as not to wake my brother. And off I would go by the light of a full moon.

I remember the first CCM stick my Dad brought home for me. I slept with it clutched in my arms.

I remember when I went away to play Junior A for the Barrie Flyers. The owner was a cheap guy and we had old equipment that

was **falling apart.** My hockey gloves were useless—they were full of holes. My Mom bought me a new pair. I was so proud to think that of all the moms that had sons on the team, the only mother who bothered to get gloves for protection was my Mom. That's Mother Love. When I look at the picture of me that still hangs in the arena in Barrie, I think of Mom and Dad and how they cared.

**Del & Maud Cherry**—they were the best. XOXO.

## don cherry

thanks, dad

for sharing

your number

with me

and for making
the room

silent

when
don cherry
is on.

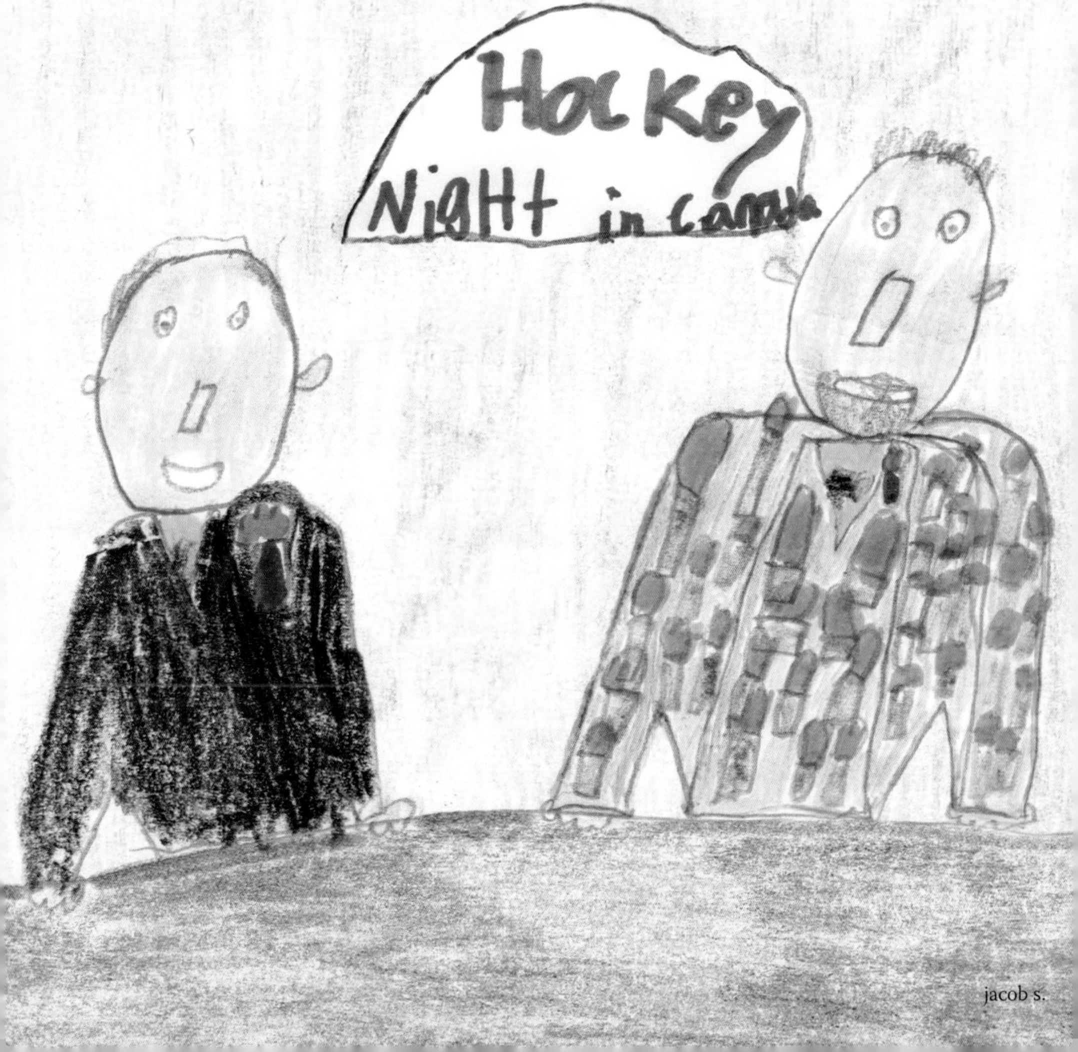


jacob s.

liam m.

thanks, dad
for driving
miles
to get me to hockey
*even* when the
roads were
closed

and once, my dad tried
to build me a huge
hockey rink in the yard
but the ice kept
melting.

liam m.

myles h.

thanks, dad
for waking
me up early

and for
agreeing with me on
which team
is going to win
when we watch NHL
on television.

myles h.

ranen d.

thanks, dad
for letting me
have fun
and giving me
time with you
all to myself

and because
you give me
tips.

# Dads hackey tips

1. keep head up.
2. Pass the puck.
3. stick handle.
4. do not body check.
5. Protect puck with bady.

thanks, dad for helping me get up

ethan d.

# when i was learning to skate

and for tying
my skates
nice and

tight.

ethan d.

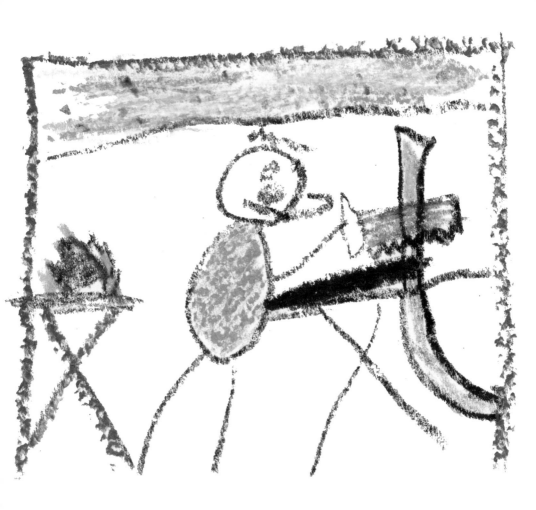

conner h.

thanks, dad
for buying my
sticks
and cutting
them with a
saw

and
*even*
for
getting
mad
at me
when
i was
lazy.

conner h.

zach v.

thanks, dad
for **playing**
end-to-end
hockey
on the driveway

and because we travel all over the place.

cade b.

thanks, dad
for driving or
walking
me to my practices
and games

cade b.

and for being the *trainer* of my hockey team.

thanks, dad

for **cheering,** pumping
me up before the games,
telling me **good job**
after the games

and he gets me
**gatorade**

and for using body signs to help me learn strategies to play... like when he flaps his arms when he's in the stands to help me remember to do the butterfly position.

ethan s.

carter t.

thanks, dad
for buying me
little blue
goalie pads
when i was a baby.
i slept with them
on and dreamed
about being a goalie

and for
making an
ice rink in the
backyard **every** winter.

sorry about the
concussion.

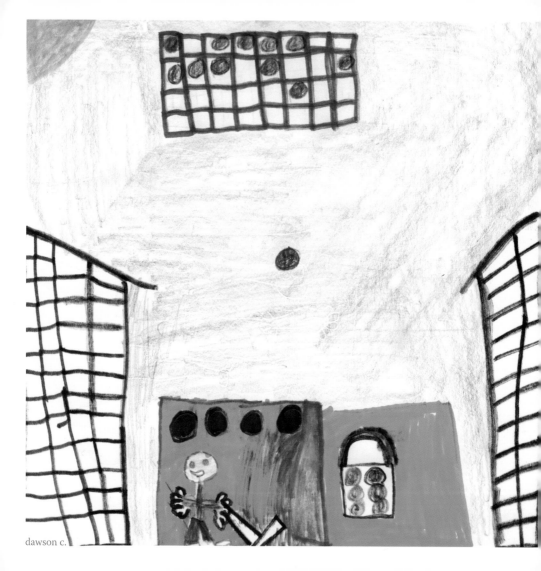

dawson c.

thanks, dad
for making me
shoot pucks
in my driveway

and once he
pumped
me up by
running the stairs
like rocky!

} *rocky iv* is my {
favourite.

dawson c.

trevor a.

thanks, dad
for teaching me how
to take shots to the
top corner

and
he
works
overtime
for
me.

trevor a.

Number
Four, Bobbyorr

richard w.

thanks, dad for reading me *number four, bobby orr!*

and once
he **showed up** at
our hockey game
**even though**
his leg was

bro ken.

thanks, dad for tying my left skate first for luck

harrison m.

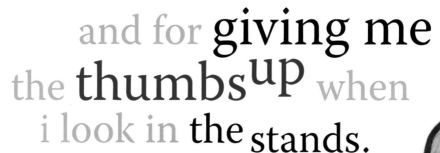

and for **giving me the thumbs**up when i look in **the** stands.

harrison m.

cameron m.

thanks, dad
for when i got to
play with you at the

father and son
game.

my
favourite
hockey player

is
you.

Thanks dad!

cameron m.

# thanks, dad
## i love you.